Poems of Swahili Proverbs

Dr Hakim Gharib Bilal

ISBN-13: 978-1522940579

ISBN-10: 152294057X

DEDICATION

This book is dedicated to my family

CONTENTS

4

1. PATIENCE BRINGS COMFORT
"Subira yavuta kheri"

Patience bring comfort
This is a real story
I may not be conversant
Regarding this theory

I may not have experience
Over this saying
However for many years
My elders had been conveying

We should always target
To get good results
However if we don't get
We should not get hurt

We should observe patience
And try another time
With good preparations
We may be lucky next time

If something is not right
Don't just give up
You might not know the results
Of what is coming up

We should be brave
And never give up
The potential we have

Will take us up

If you are disappointed
For one reason or another
Observe patience
To take you further

If you are not happy
From any results
Patience is the therapy
To calm your heart

If you are in trouble
Or facing defeat
Be very humble
And try to solve it

I must admit
In certain situation
It is very difficult
To observe patience

This is the only way
To be able to cope
In a global highway
Don't lose hope

There is nobility
And also brave
Patience is the quality
Which good people have

2. LITTLE BY LITTLE FILL MEASURES
"Haba na haba hujaza kibaba"

Nothing is too little
And insignificant
It is a matter of filling it
To achieve what you want

The little measure is something
That is all I want to say
Better compared with nothing
It is just a matter of days

If you have some money
And deposit somewhere
While keep on adding
For a number of years

You will not be disappointed
By the time drawn
The money you deposited
Has really grown

This does not only apply to money
But also other things
We start with number one
And ended up with something

Billions are not billions
But numbers before them
They could be millions

Or even thousands

Don't look down on things
Which are very little
They tend to fill
What you didn't expect

Don't look down on things
That are very rare
They can be big
And make you scare

It is not only mathematic
Which I'm referring
The real life tricks
Is what we should be worrying

It is not secret
In our development
We should be consistent
With our achievements

A small accumulation
May not be significant
But in many years duration
It has a big impact

Small drops
May not be significant
If they don't stop
They can fill a tank

It is from history
And also experience
Small unknown companies
Have become giants

Whatever you are planning
You should aim high
If nothing is forthcoming
Give another try

Even a small step
As you climb up
Just maintain the gape
And never give up

3. BLOOD IS HAVIER THAN WATER
"Damu nzito kuliko maji"

Obviously blood is heavier
Than the same amount of water
Since it has a bigger share
Of different matters

If you take measurement
And calculate the density
You will see the difference
About the reality

This is a rough meaning

Of this expression
Which has a deeper meaning
More than we can mention

It is not just what you hear
And find the meaning
This proverb adhere
To the cultural understanding

In Swahili culture
Many will agree
The family structure
Is a big tree

We deeply value
All the blood relation
Uncles and whoever who
Are considered special

In Swahili culture
The family is deeply rooted
Whether sister or brother
No one is forgotten

Because of this
Blood is heavier than water
Such a relationship
Is all that matter

This mentality
Should not be viewed as rude

The general hospitality
Of Swahili people is good

Their attitude
Is always positive
Even with less food
They are ready to give

What I am trying to mention
Should be clearly understood
Swahilis greatly appreciate
Their brotherhood

This is very true
In many world cultures
The family bond is good
And care for one others

4. KINDNESS IS NEVER LOST
"Wema hauwozi"

Kindness is never lost
I believe in that
If you played a host
Don't think that has past

It is kept somewhere
Waiting to come back
You may not be aware
Of such a feedback

You will see it back
Knocking on your door
When you are desperate
In your daily chores

You will be surprised
With the sequence of events
Or get a prize
Which you never intend

Kindness is like investment
You keep it for yourself
All the goodness are kept
Right on the shelf

Properly secured
With an added value
A good multiplier
Of more than two

No depreciation
On what you will get
Your kind actions
Has no regret

No bankruptcy
Or bad outcome
Be kind and easy
You will be free from harms

Deposit as much as you can
To any one in need
Life is like a train
It slows and speed

Don't expect a gift
Or any return
Just continue to give
And God has a plan

During this time
Someone is vulnerable
Don't use your kind
To ask for impossible

Kindness is such a thing
You can help any
It may seem nothing
Not even a penny

The timing is important
When you help someone
The urgency of the matter
Become number one

It will happen to you
One day in this world
You will need kindness too
From someone unheard

This world is round

And keep on rotating
What goes around
Can touch any being

We are in a small village
The like of this world
Everybody should be treated
In the best way we can afford

Because we don't know
When is our fate
Life is such a show
Everybody participate

Because we don't know
What will happen to us
Today or tomorrow
There may be a task

5. THERE IS NO SMOKE WITHOUT FIRE
"Penye moshi pana moto"

Smoke is a warning
Of something big
The fire maybe burning
And spoil everything

It may not be significant
By just seeing a smoke
People may not want

To even take a note

How thick is the smoke
This may be a factor
It could be from exhaust
Something which doesn't matter

It could be from firewood
Someone has set up
Whoever is preparing food
It doesn't matter

Or a big fire
Like a burning house
The smoke will appear
Absolutely no doubt

Therefore we should be mindful
When there is smoke
Something harmful
May cause havoc

In certain circumstances
You cannot see the fire
You will have to open
Almost everywhere

Or to dig down
Under the ashes
The fire can be found
With red hot flushes

The smoke maybe troublesome
In certain ways
It can kill someone
Who comes its way

The fire is even scarier
And cause more harms
We should always be aware
With possible outcomes

The smoke is like a warning
Of what may come
It keeps informing
Of the possible harms

When we see a smoke
We shouldn't ignore
Unless we know the source
And the fire is no more

The most practical way
Is to monitor the smoke
If it comes our way
We should not take it as a joke

6. OUT OF SIGHT OUT OF MIND
"Asiyekuwepo na lake halipo"

The mind cannot imagine
What the eyes cannot see

This proverb is genuine
Most people will agree

The sight of something
Is a good reminder
Of what is missing
In previous agenda

The sight of someone
Is like an identity
To consider in your plan
And give him a priority

It shows he cares
So much about the event
That is why he is there
Without being late

If there is anything
To be distributed
He will get something
Undisputed

If there is something
Which has to be given
He will get something
No matter when

He will have a share
Whether small or big
Because he is there

To negotiate the bid

If you want to be noticed
Don't just sit behind
Choose a front sit
And speak your mind

However talk wisely
And speak the truth
Don't hurt people's feeling
And those close to you

Your being onsite
Should be beneficial
And people will like
Your great contribution

Don't just be there
For the sake of it
And claim your share
Without working for it

7. CLOUDS ARE SIGNS OF RAIN
"Dalili ya mvuwa mawingu"

Clouds are first to be seen
Before rain start
It is like a routine
Anywhere on earth

You can almost predict
When it is going to rain
When clouds are thick
And cover the plain

It does not need a genius
It is a matter of when
When the clouds are obvious
Expect the rain

When you see the clouds
Get your umbrella
Whether you go to town
Or just around your area

When you are driving
That is fine
Watch out on arriving
You might face the rain

When you are in-door
Or working in the office
You may not hear the downpour
Just enjoy your coffee.

It is quite true
The clouds could be anything
Which gives a clue
Something will be happening

It is almost impossible

To have it rain
When the weather is good
And the skies are plain

The rain cannot come
All of a sudden
Without the presence of clouds
And sometimes thunders

8. BETTER LATE THAN NEVER
"Kawia ufike"

We tend to be in a hurry
As we drive in our areas
Occasionally ignoring
The warnings which are there

We tend to speed
In a highway
Not taking a heed
Of what the signs say

Overtaking with carelessness
Can cause problem
A lot of accidents
Were caused by them

Haste is the main reason
And rushing somewhere
Your life is precious

Please be aware

We must arrive safely
Rather than otherwise
As we drive daily
That is the advice

It is better to be late
Than not arriving
To be announced dead
While we were driving

We will not be doing justice
Even to our families
Disturbing the traffic
From our hurries

We will not be fair
Even to ourselves
We should be aware
And discipline ourselves

We won't be fair
To the traffic flows
We should also fear
To break the law

In a nutshell
This is my conclusion
We should drive well
To avoid collision

Slowly is the way
As long as we arrive
We should not play
With our dear life

9. A BAD COCONUT RENDERS GOOD ONES BAD
"Nazi mbovu harabu ya nzima"

This is a statement
About general items
To apply judgment
On issues which are related

It is like a random check
On certain items
If you find fake
Not fit to be eaten

Or when a sample is taken
For quality assurance
We know what happen
For the test in question

When one coconut is bad
It is well understood
The rest will be discarded
Even though they are good
The image of the company

Or any organization
Is reflected to the public
By the leaders in question

Or the representatives
And their reputation
The public are attentive
And watch their action

It is not a healthy mind
To criticized people
According to their kind
Or principles

It is not a good idea
To generalized people
According to what we hear
Or just a gossip

It may be unfair
For us to conclude
By checking a single pair
And say nothing is good

There are other example
I don't want to mention
Generalized on people
According to their nation

Giving a bad name
Which spoil their reputation

Just because a few of them
Belong to certain faction

Giving a bad name
And tannish their image
Because a few of them
Behaves inhuman

10. WHERE THERE IS A WILL THERE IS A WAY
"Penye nia pana njia"

All the actions
You are planning to do
Depend on the intention
Coming from you

It is like a proposal
Of certain project
Written by the author
To achieve the target

It is very strange
To embark on project
Without a proper plan
And expect it to be perfect

The will is important
To initiate the plan
The project can start

Once preparations are done

This will help our brain
To stay in focus
And help to maintain
What is important

You will clear the bush
And make a way
You don't need to push
Everything is ok

You can make foundation
Even on the hill
You can see progression
If there is a will

You will not meet obstruction
If you have a will
There will be a solution
Right under your heel

The will is important
In everything we do
We should not be ignorant
And do what we do

11.BIRDS OF THE SAME FEATHERS FLOCK TOGETHER
"Ndege wa aina moja huruka pamoja"

Birds of the same feathers
Have a lot in common
They know each other
In every corner

They fly together
Wherever they go
In front are the leaders
Who seemed to know

They eat common food
Although they don't share
In such a mood
Nobody is scared

Characters are the same
Just like twins
You cannot separate them
The way they sing

They share habitat
Or common settlements
They don't have contracts
Just informal agreement

Or just convenience
For their own safety

To help in defense
Of their big party

They have a social order
And a ranking protocol
The young and the elders
They work for all

They have a high discipline
Of doing things together
Nothing come in between
To spoil their feathers

They live in harmony
And common understanding
Enjoying their company
With wonderful things

People who know them
Cannot differentiate
Behaviors are the same
Even the way they dress

For birds of migration
Who fly to different continents
They have a common mission
Known to each of them

People with same habits
Are likely to be together
They share the tis bits

And all the fun together

They share the food
Whatever it is
In such a good mood
Call it a feast

They understands one another
No matter where
The color of their feathers
Remove all the barriers

Anyone who is different
Will leave the flock
Will feel out of place
And take a different walk

The difference in behaviors
Or attitude
Create a barrier
In brotherhood

The difference in talk
Or eating habit
Create a joke
For others to take it

This is a big lesson
For those who understand
Birds of the same feathers
Are likely to be friends

Since they are together
For good or bad
Birds of the same feathers
Are like friends

And those who are different
Away will fly
Taking with them
The ones of their like

With their own celebrations
And cut all the bonds
Not even invitation
As they are on their own

12.TOO MANY COOKS SPOIL THE BROTH
"Wapishi wengi huharibu mchuzi"

It is a must
In everything we do
The leadership should first
Consider everyone's view

With too many leaders
It is not easy
To execute orders
Or to form a policy

The broth is cooked

With different spices
Measured with spoon
Of different sizes

It could be a table spoon
To make a full measure
Or even a cup full
There may be confusion

The type of broth
Should be clearly mentioned
Ingredients brought forth
And timely added

Individual ingredients
Which suites the test
Poured in measurement
And cooked to the best

Estimation of salts
Should be well understood
No room for faults
For the food to be good

The chef who cook
Should be well known
Who can prepare food
The best in town

Customer satisfaction
Who have come to eat

Depend on the vision
The chef has on it

This is all possible
If we have one good chef
Aware of the edibles
In the kitchen shelf

If there are many cooks
In one kitchen
Preparing the same food
What will happened

The kitchen will be in mess
And the broth spoiled
With salt in excess
And water spilled

The broth is an example
In this Swahili statement
It is very applicable
In many life environment

There can't be two presidents
Or two prime ministers
We will be overloaded
With differing matters

We will be confused
Of whom to follow
As we are not used

With such portfolios

This reminds me
Of another proverb
About the lorry
With many drivers

Or about the boat
With many bosses
It will just float
And get lost

There must be discipline
And maintenance of the mood
Instructions coming in
Must be well understood

There must be a leader
The president or the like
With good general orders
Everybody will like

There must be a boss
In charge for all
Who can prepare broth
Eaten by all

13.A PERSON MISSING THIS HAS THAT
"Mso hili ana lile"

This is another proverb
Swahilis like to say
Everybody is important
In his own way

Here is a good lesson
In this Swahili saying
We shouldn't look down
To any human being

Someone maybe clever
In performing certain task
He can work over and over
To get the best results

However he may be slow
In performing other tasks
He may even not know
Which comes first

He may not have understanding
About other business
Although he is outstanding
In doing what he does.

We tend to be specialists
In our own fields
And know the least

Of the other world

We tend to concentrate
On what we know best
And always forget
About the rest

This is human nature
As we all know
We are always pressured
With our own chores

We should develop a passion
Of appreciating others
To love their profession
Or whatever their business

We should not look down
On other specialties
They are on their own
An important faculty

We are all best
In what we do
Let us concentrate
For our best of views

14. IF YOU DON'T SEAL A CRACK, YOU WILL END UP BUILDING A WALL
"Usipoziba ufa utajenga ukuta"

Crack is a sign
Of weakness on the wall
Things are not fine
And the building might fall

We should not ignore
And pretend it is not there
We may lose the wall
If the crack is not repaired

This is part of us
We human beings
We tend to be smart
And forget small things

Accumulated problems
Becomes complicated
A solution to them
May give you a headache

We had enough time
To make amendments
Cracks can cause harm
If done too late

We can make it better
Right from the beginning

Or correct the matter
Before becoming chronic

Identify the mistake
Before the wall fall
Repair the crack
Once and for all

It is a preventive attitude
To train our mind
Good for our livelihood
And every kind

You will not regret
With this mentality
You will be great
In your faculty

You will be on top of the problem
Steering the right way
Watching for it to happen
And clear it right away

The earlier the crack is repaired
The better for the building
With little resources to spare
This is the best dealing

15.A FRIEND INNEED IS A FRIEND INDEED
"Akufaae kwa dhiki ndiye rafiki"

This is a simple proverb
And easy to understand
Its meaning is straight forward
Right to the end

A friend during the need
Is a genuine friend
They always take a heed
And care to the end

When you are in trouble
Or in any hardship
They are the first people
To come for your help

They don't care
How much you have
They are only there
To give you help

They regard humanity
As far more important
Racial and ethnicity
It doesn't matter

They regard life
As most precious

And always strive
In their friendly mission

To them a friend is a friend
Whoever she or he can be
And ready to defend
Come what it maybe

They give whatever help
To their dear friend
Advice or even wealth
Whatever comes hands

They don't mind at all
To help a needy friend
Be it one or all
They will always give a hand

They are not the individual
Who are selfish
Who only like someone
For their own benefit

They are not individual
Who hate each other
And like to do harm
To one another

Their mutual benefit
Is without contract
They do what it fit

To keep in contact

The problem of one
Is known to the other
Even for fun
They joke each other

The ones who don't care
Are not friends
They are only there
For their own errands

16.A CHILLI PAPER YOU HAVEN'T EATEN HOW COULD IT MAKE YOU HOT?
"Pilipili usoila inakuwashia nini"?

A chili is hot
When you bite it for a trying
If you are very soft
You will end up crying

Your mouth will be burning
With a hot sensation
Chili is number one
In spice competition

You should not feel anything
If you don't touch it
Why are you complaining
You are away from it

If it fall in your food
And accidentally eat it
It will be understood
If you complain about it

But if it is far away
Not even in neighborhood
And you complain anyway
That will not be good

We should not be bothered
For issues not involved
Leave it to others
Who know how to solve

We should not interfere
With other people's issues
Unless it is clear
They want to hear from you

Whatever people talk
If about themselves
We shouldn't be provoked
That will not help

Whatever people do
Whether good or bad
If it does not concern you
Just turn your head

Sometimes it is difficult
To keep quiet
If someone is hurt
And you are there

Use your discretion
And see what you can do
Remember your mission
To help others too

17. WHAT EATS YOU IS IN YOUR DRESS
"Kikulacho kinguoni mwako"

When something happen to you
Don't look for the culprit
Just look around you
To see what is it

When something happened to anyone
He shouldn't look far
It could be from someone
Who is even closer

If something happened to us
We should check on ourselves
There is no need to rush
It is the attitude we have

If anything happened to them
Which can bring sorrow

They have no one to blame
It is their own shadow

Ask yourself first
What actually happened
Things from your past
May have the hand

Scrutinize yourself
And those close to you
The problem you have
Could be harming you

Those close to you
Who are your advisers
Informing you
Things you shouldn't bother

It could be the attitude
Which is very bad
People close to you
Cannot withstand

It could be the manners
Which are not tolerable
Destroying your honors
And put you in trouble

It could be your actions
Counter productive
Destroying your mission

Of being proactive
Don't blame others
For your bad luck
Look no further
It's your own heart

Don't blame people
For your down fall
Your own principles
Have created a hole

Don't blame the world
For your non-starter
Just check your words
You need to be smarter

18.A PERSON WHO DIG WELL GET HIMSELF INSIDE FIRST
"Mchimba kisima huingia mwenyewe"

Digging a traditional well
Uses basic tools
There is no other way
The digger enter too

This is a manual work
Which is labor intensive
The digger has to work
Right from the deep

As he dig down
Every minute matter
He will not sit down
Until he sees water

This is a direct meaning
Of this proverb
In the well digging
The diggers will enter first

This is not tell
As we will see
The digger of the well
Could be any human being

Who is plotting something
Against society
He will be the first victim
Of his conspiracy

We shouldn't do anything
That is harmful
They will end up bouncing
And hit us too

No more bad feeling
No more bad intention
We should facilitate healing
Rather than confrontation

19.THE BEST FINGER GET A RING
"Chanda chema huvikwa pete"

The ring is a precious item
Given with special reserve
The finger is one of them
As long as it deserve

It is like a gift
For outstanding performance
The ring is not cheap
It may cost thousands

Not only in value
But also psychology
The ring actual value
Cannot be imagined

It is a normal thing
For many cultures
To give special ring
For special occasions

It should be considered
In such a manner
Among so many fingers
Which one should be honored

It may not be easy
Given the environment

They may all be busy
For the best achievement

The question may arise
Which finger should be chosen
For the best prize
Which suites them

The most deserving one
Should be carefully picked
Who will be the one
To deserve the gift

All the example mentioned
Represent societies
People who are talented
Are given special priorities

Those who contributed
Greatly in their nation
Their actions are noted
With utmost recognition

They are highly rewarded
And given encouragement
With proper guidance
To extend their achievement

After all
They are the most favored
Giving their all

For their best endeavors

They are the best fingers
Picked by the owner
Their reward is bigger
Since they are winners

20.TO AIM IS NOT TO HIT
"Kuelekeza siyo kufuma"

To aim is not to hit
We all know
If someone boast of it
We should just ignore

We should not cheat ourselves
Or pretend it
The things we have
We made it

We cannot be champion
Because we aimed it
The real heroes
Are the ones who make a hit

In a football match
Or any other game
To hit is a must
And not just to aim

In a dart game
The same rule applies
You must aim
And score high

You can't be joyful
Just because you aimed
You need to show people
Of your fame

If you want to be a celebrity
Just show people how
It is not just politics
But actions somehow

People want to see
The project implementation
They will not be pleased
For any in action

We should fulfil
Whatever we promised
Written in detail
With nothing missed

We should show people
Our intention
Of solving issued
Already mentioned

Then we will be winning

The people heart
By not just aiming
But hit the target

21.FOLD THE FISH WHILE STILL FRESH
"Samaki mkunje bado mbichi"

When you want to fold the fish
Do it while fresh
This is their trick
Soon after the catch

A freshly caught fish
Is very flexible
You can easily fold it
With minimum trouble

On either direction
You can try
The fish can be fashioned
Before it dry

On either side
You can manipulate
By the time it's dry
It is be too late

On right or left
It is possible
You can manipulate

Without trouble

On either side
You can bend
Left or right
Depend on the trend

Don't try to wait
Until too late
You may not be able to get
What you anticipate

You will be tempted to wait
And not to try
The fish will break
When it is dry

It can happen to people
Such as young children
Training is simple
Just direct them

The earlier the better
It becomes a habit
Children are smatter
To easily adopt it

As they are flexible
Like a fresh fish
They can easily be able
To learn with ease

They are easily trainable
With new ideas
Their mood understandable
Without fear

22.WHEN YOU SEE THEM AFLOAT SOMEBODY MADE THEM
"Ukiona vyaelea vimeumbwa"

This is another example
The Swahilis have spoken
It is not that simple
As it is written

It is not easy
To make a floating object
Some principles of Physics
With some good knowledge

It could be a human being
Who is knowledgeable
Applied engineering
To make the ship floatable

Or a good designer
Who manufacture a boat
And make it in a manner
For it to float

We can say the same
For a beautiful Villa
It just never came
And raised without pillars

The same can be said
About aircraft
Flying without aid
With no hiccups

Everything under the sun
From far and beyond
Created by One
Who knows no bound

Fashioned to perfection
With no faults
The best creations
With no doubt

Seeing floating vessels
Is very wonderful
The kind of innovation
Is remarkable

Made of steel and iron
Yet its space is ample
Traditionally admired
By our local people

For an object to float

That is superb
The Swahilis they thought
To make a proverb

It is just an example
Of general expression
Which is applicable
In many narrations

When you see them afloat
They are created
A ship or a boat
Or any other vessel

23.NOT EVERYTHING WHICH GLITTER IS GOLD
"Kila king'aracho si dhahabu"

Gold is a precious metal
Many people like it
With a feeling good factor
Who can hate it?

It is a precious element
Mostly for decorations
With all the good complements
History has mentioned

It's value is high
Is a sign of prosperity

It can easily buy
Any valuable commodity

Many have account
Right in the bank
There is no doubt
About this fact

It is like money
When it comes to exchange
Gold is number one
To be put in bank

Due to those factors
Gold had been mentioned
In Swahili chapters
As a metal of fashion

It is well known
The way it glitters
Gold is number one
Among the heavy metals

We should be careful
In this modern age
Things can fool
Even to the best judges

Not all which glitter is gold
Many of us knew
Not just because we were told

But this is the general view

The truth will remain
Forever and ever
No one can complain
About this proverb

All which glitter is not gold
The elders already saw
This is the nature of the world
We should all know

It could be a cheap metal
With good painting
Decorated in such a pattern
Or just the outer coating

The way it glitters
You can't differentiate
It is just a cheap metal
With an outer paint

The same applies to human
Who are not what they are
They call now and then
To show how good they are

They pretend to be good
To get people's respect
Smiling in such a mood
No one can suspect

After a few weeks
Everything will be clear
Their dirty tricks
Will start to appear

The artificial sheep skin
Will soon come off
With a different human being
Just like a wolf

We should be careful
In our everyday affairs
Such type of people
Are not what they appear

They maybe shining
Like a gold bar
Everything is running
The way they are

Pretend to be good
To get what they want
And change their mood
To the original one

Their true pattern
That of old
Which is neither glitter
Nor is gold

This is the advice
From our very old
All glittering devices
Cannot be gold

24.ONE FINGER CANNOT KILL A LOUSE
"Kidole kimoja hakivunji chawa"

One finger alone
Can do nothing
It needs another one
To hold on something

One finger alone
Is less effective
When it comes to perform
Important duties

It is only possible
When in teamwork
The finger will be able
To do what it want

Unity is the strength
The opposite is weakness
The finger of the hand
Should work in togetherness

The same for us people
In our everyday actions

Unity may triple
The results of our actions

We should not be alone
And allow segregation
The best outcome
Is not from isolation

We should work together
Hand in hand
To overcome the weather
This is the trend

If fingers can
Then it should be possible
To work hand in hand
To achieve the impossible

25. WHERE THERE ARE TREES THERE ARE NO BUILDERS
"Penye miti hapana wajenzi"

In Swahili culture
Trees were used for buildings
Modified for construction
With proper soiling

Many trees fell
Because of that
As construction went well

More trees were cut

The trees were associated
With housing construction
In any location
That was the assumption

When few trees are found
It may be difficult
People have to move around
To build their huts

Where there are many trees
Builders are not there
The forest will be free
With no reason to clear

We always take things
For granted
Where there are opportunities
There is no one to take

This is an example
Of this Swahili saying
It is just a sample
Of what it implying

I may not be exact
Of the actual meaning
And I may not be perfect
In explaining

Where there are plenty
No one to take
Where there is scarcity
Everyone want to get

This is the summation
Of what I could say
In this expression
Of this Swahili Say

26.THERE IS NO SECRET BETWEEN TWO PEOPLE
"Hakuna siri ya watu wawili"

The secret of the secret
Is not to share
There should not be witness
In any of the affairs

We should be careful
On any chit-chat
This is the secret rule
If anything like that

Depend on the situation
The secret can be safe
A close relation
Your secret can have

You might need a witness
In certain assignment
You cannot keep a secret
To avoid disappointment

Whatever happen
Think of the outcome
Of the secret in question
And how to overcome

We should always weigh
The pros and the cons
Of what we say
And the secret concern

Bearing in mind
Of this fact
Only in your mind
Lies the best secret

27.ANGER BRINGS LOSS
"Hasira hasara"

Anger is not good
It can damage your homes
The decision in such a mood
Has bad outcomes

It should be best avoided
In every situation

It is preloaded
With no brain function

There may be no reasoning
When it comes to anger
Whatever happening
Is a potential danger

It can damage you
And close people
This is true
With many examples

Anger control
Should be exercised
It is effective overall
And the best advice

Lest we should fall
With bad judgment
Anger control
Is the best treatment

Lest we should suffer
With a big loss
Anger can only offer
A false hope

Lest we incur
A big damage
Anger can offer

Nothing to salvage

28.To STUMBLE IS NOT TO FALL
"Kujikwaa siyo kuanguka"

To stumble is not to fall
This is the reality
Continue with your goal
To improve the quality

It is a small hiccup
Not worth a penny
You can easily pick up
To continue the journey

Stumbling is any obstacle
Which can come your way
It can be a vehicle
To make your mission delay

It can come in between
As you implement your plan
Just keep on doing
No matter hard it can

Your stumbling should not be a vehicle
To abandon your mission
Just identify the obstacle
To reach your vision

Don't feel sorry
You have not fall yet
Continue with your story
Until you achieve the best

Don't regret
For a mere stumbling
You will get the best
If you keep on running

Keep on planning
If not running
A small stumbling
Should not make you panic

29.A PROMISE IS DEBT
"Ahadi ni deni"

Promise is debt
Which has to be fulfilled
This is a general concept
Not just in Swahili

Promise is debt
No doubt about it
The message we get
We should practice it

We should not make promise

If we cannot fulfil it
People will take a notice
And waiting for it

If you can't make it
They might be angry
They will keep on asking
To get to the real story

If you can't make it
They will not be pleased
They will keep on mentioning it
And make you unease

They will be disappointed
To say the least
All your efforts wasted
To win people's heart

Truth should be known
Right from the beginning
Whatever is shown
Promise should not be in the dealing

If it is not possible
It should be stated earlier
Promise can be liable
To agreement failure

As for politicians
In their provinces

They should have vision
And not just promises

As for most people
In their daily walk
They should be careful
In their talk

As for most people
In their daily service
They should mindful
With their promise

30.HE WHO DOES NOT ADMIT DEFEAT IS NOT A COMPETITOR
"Asiyekubali kushindwa si mshindani"

In any competition
There are certain facts
With only two options
Winning or losing the match

We are all aware
Right from the beginning
When we enter the stadium
It is either loosing or winning

There is no third option
Or alternatives
In any competition

There are clear directives

It is either the looser
Or the winner
There is no other
In sport arena

Everyone should accept
Right before the event
He may not be the best
Right to the end

We should accept the results
Whatever they maybe
We may be hurt
But let it be

We should congratulate the winner
And shake their hands
In such a manner
We are still friends

Maybe next time
We can still compete
And emerge number one
And avoid defeat

Those who can't accept defeat
Should not be in the match
They cannot compete
With such a mindset

They can spoil the match
And cause mischief
No one can tolerate
And ask them to leave

We cannot entertain
Such group of people
What they want to maintain
Is against the principles

To admit a defeat
Is part of the game
Nothing new about it
The rules are the same

There is no meaning
Of having special man
Who are always winning
By virtue of their clan

It is not good
To play a game
When the governing rules
Are not the same

Winning the game
Or losing one
The rules are the same
For everyone

31.THE REAL EATER IS TODAY'S EATER NOT YESTERDAY
"Mla mla leo mla jana kala nini?"

In case you are wondering
About those who ate yesterday
It is nothing comparing
To those who eat today

You might have experience
From yesterday's food
But why today you are here
If your stomach was full

You can't be full
Since you ate yesterday
The norm of the food
Is to be eaten everyday

You will be busy
And not in the mood
Opening fridges
Searching for food

To eat is today
Yesterday is history
You are hungry anyway
What is your story

We should not be boastful
And feel good

The smell of yesterday's food
Has disappeared for good

Some have forgotten
And lost appetite
The food they have eaten
Was an old bite

You might have eaten yesterday
And that is true
But you are still hungry today
What to do?

Yesterday was important
To be able to understand
To analyze the matter
According to what happened

We should concentrate on future
And think of what to do
History is just a teacher
To know what was true

We should be mindful
And look ahead
Yesterday was eventful
But maybe too late

Eating today
Is a better idea
Ok for yesterday

But who really care?

If you give me a choice
Of when to eat
I will vote twice
For today's meat

The winner is today
No doubt about it
Everyone will be ok
To have a slice of it

Yesterday's choice
Is not a favorite
We need to think twice
Before we eat

32.Every bird flies with its own wing
"Kila ndege huruka kwa ubawa wake"

A bird cannot fly
Without wings
Even if it tries
It won't succeed

They should be related
To their weight
To be able to take them
To a great height

It should be of their own
And not from someone
So as to keep on
Flying with fun

To fly everywhere
On its own mission
It doesn't have to care
Or asking for permission

Its meaning is broad
Especially for human
Talking about the bird
We need to explain

People have different abilities
To do certain tusk
The difference in life quality
Reflect on that

We cannot rely on someone's tool
For our job
It is of different school
To fit our job

We cannot bet
On someone's fortune
To achieve success
That is not a rule

33.Savings never go bad
"Akiba haiozi"

In a real life situation
We have to keep saving
This is a good suggestion
To avoid starving

Be it for us
Or the future generation
Saving for us
Is not just a pension

Always the advantages
Out weight the risk
Saving for old age
No need to think

Not just in currency
But other items
Whose value is easy
To trace them

Savings never go bad
Most will agree
Whatever you had
Will set you free

You will realize later
When you need it
Saving really matter

When you have nothing to eat

34. The one who wants what is under the bed must stoop for it
"Mtaka cha mvunguni huinama"

To get something under the bed
You have to stoop for it
The only alternative one have
Is to lift it

It's all about being humble
When we ask for something
It is a general principle
The way we do things

When you are in school
It is not just about the knowledge
Humility is the rule
To take you to the edge

Anything under the bed
Be ready to bend
The only way you can have
What you really intend

Lifting the bed
Is not a gentle way
The impact it has
Will keep your luck away

We should use persuasion
Rather than force
In a good application
There is nothing worse

Maintain humility
And being humble
No matter your identity
You will be successful

35.A sugarcane is sweetest at the joint "Utamu wa muwa kifundoni"

Success is enjoyed better
If it comes from ourselves
It is not an outside matter
And done with no help

It is our own effort
Which we really appreciate
It shows how smart
Things can get

We played a big part
In the development
The joy in our heart
With such achievement

This is a big motivation
To encourage ourselves
The big celebration

Comes from what we have

Encourage self-reliance
In any possible way
Even forming alliance
Is not far away

Then we can appreciate
The fruits of our actions
And what we get
Job satisfaction

36.Going infront does not mean arriving at the destination
"Kutangulia si kufika"

Going in front
Is a good beginning
It is a good start
For your winning

Going in front
Is not a condition
To be where you want
In your mission

Not even a condition
To reach the destination
During the mission
Anything can happen

Don't be boasting
That you are ahead
The race is just starting
You will end up being sad

Don't pretend
That you are ahead
You may not reach the end
Let alone to lead

Don't be proud
You are in front
A boastful sound
Will not give you what you want

To reach a place
Depends on many things
Not just a pace
And who is starting

If someone is ahead
We don't say he has arrived
He has just take a lead
And maybe he will survive

37.When the cat is away the mouse play
"Paka akiondoka panya hutawala"

When the cat is away
This is quite obvious

The mouse will play
And be joyous

They will move freely
In their movement
And very unwilling
In their engagement

They dare do anything
If the cat is away
And mess everything
Which comes their way

They are not scared
Of anybody else
Who could inject fear
And destroy their face

The cat is like a boss
Or a king
Who can easily use force
To make things working

Where there is no boss
Or a leader
The company will be in loss
With no order

Made in the USA
Las Vegas, NV
06 July 2022